What Was It Like?™
THOMAS EDISON

by Michael Weinberg
illustrated by George Ford

Longmeadow Press

Published by Longmeadow Press
201 High Ridge Road, Stamford, CT 06904

ANGEL
ENTERTAINMENT·INC

Manufactured in the United States of America.

My name is Thomas Edison and I was an inventor for most of my life. You've probably even used some of my most famous inventions, such as the light bulb and the phonograph. Anyway, it always seemed unfair to me that people thought the word "inventor" meant a crazy-looking person in a long white coat who mixes weird potions in a laboratory. I don't think I was ever like *that*, although the man who inspired me to become an inventor absolutely was!

They called Sam Winchester the "Mad Miller of Milan," which was the name of the small town in Ohio where we lived. Mr. Winchester earned his living by grinding wheat into flour in his gristmill. People said, though, that there was another place in his mill where he did all sorts of mysterious things.

I don't know how you felt about mysteries when you were five years old, but I can tell you how I felt. I wanted to find out exactly what those other things were. When my mother warned me to stay away from the mill, that just made me want to go there even more.

The one other place that Mama told me I shouldn't go was the town's canal. I wanted to be a good boy, but sometimes I just couldn't see the sense in Mama's rules. So, when I got tired of dangling my feet over the canal, and when there were no more barges for me to wave to, I decided it was time to find out about those mysterious other things.

One day, I sneaked through the open door of the mill. Then, I got down on my hands and knees and crept very quietly behind a big wooden grain bin. From my hiding place, I could see a tall man with wild gray hair and bushy white eyebrows—the miller! He was working over a long, low table. His hands were moving quickly, and he was talking to himself. He didn't look crazy to me—he looked like he was having fun!

I didn't dare move closer to see just what the miller was tinkering with, but I couldn't miss the huge yellow piece of canvas stretched out on the floor beside his bench. There was a straw basket on the floor, too. It wasn't a picnic basket, though, unless two thousand people were planning to put their lunch in there!

While I was asking myself what in the world such things could be used for, the miller looked in the direction of my hiding place. I don't know if he saw me crouching behind that bin or not, but I was too scared to sit still and find out! I jumped up and ran out of the mill as fast as my legs would carry me. I was halfway home before I reminded myself that I still hadn't discovered what the miller was doing. I made up my mind that no matter how scared I was, I would go back every day until I found out.

The next morning was sunny, so I decided to sit by the canal before heading for the mill. The water looked so nice that I thought I might take a dip and see if I could teach myself how to swim. That couldn't be too dangerous. I was sure that I was much too lightweight to drown!

Suddenly, I heard a tremendous roar. That noise probably saved my life. Instead of jumping into the water, where I would have sunk like a stone, I turned around and saw a great cloud of smoke rising from the mill. I realized that it had caught fire and suddenly exploded.

I ran, but by the time I got there it had burned halfway to the ground. The miller was standing on one side of the road looking dazed. Folks from our town were standing on the other side, shaking their heads and saying to each other, "We'd better watch out or that crazy fool will blow up the world!"

Listening to the grown-ups talking, I finally found out what the miller had been doing with that yellow canvas and the huge basket. He was making a balloon to carry passengers across Lake Erie, the big lake our town bordered. "A balloon," folks said, "how foolish. He could have killed himself!"

A balloon, I thought, how wonderful! If only he hadn't set fire to the mill while he was putting it together, he could have flown to the moon. I hope he tries again!

Years later, after my family had moved to a different town, I heard that the miller *had* tried again. He'd built a second balloon, and this one had worked!

Before anyone could congratulate the Mad Miller, though, he climbed into his balloon, waved good-bye and flew away over Lake Erie. No one heard from him again, and most people figured that his balloon had crashed and he had drowned in the lake. But it seems to me that a man who could build a balloon all by himself could also get to anyplace he wanted to go. I think that the miller just found somewhere else to live on the other side of the lake, and decided ay where people wouldn't call him crazy.

When I was seven years old, we moved to Port Huron, Michigan, on the shore of Lake Huron. When the winter wind blew off that big lake, I'd get a chill that rose from the tips of my toes to the top of my head. The first few months we lived there, I was so sick that my mother seldom let me get out of bed.

I hated staying alone. Our new house was next to an old, dark army cemetery. As I lay in bed, I imagined that the noises the wind made were the moans and groans of the ghosts of dead soldiers rising up out of their graves!

When I began feeling better, my folks told me that it was time I started school. Our school-house had only one classroom, where children of all different grades and ages sat together. There were so many of us in that one room that if we all began to talk and ask questions, it made a terrible racket. Well, Reverend Engle, our teacher, did not like noise. He believed that children should only speak when they are spoken to. Every day he carried a long wooden cane, and if you said one word without being called on, he would whack you with that big stick right across the behind.

Now, that wasn't exactly what I thought school should be like. There were all kinds of questions buzzing around in my head about what made the planets move and what electricity was. But it seemed that the only thing old Reverend Engle really wanted to teach me was how to keep quiet and behave.

Reverend Engle was disappointed in me, too, and I had the cane marks to prove it. He never seemed to notice how much I wanted to learn. All he knew was that when I wasn't fidgeting in my seat or looking out the window, I was talking and making noise.

One day, when the Reverend was showing some visitors around the school, he pointed to me and said very loudly, "That boy will never amount to anything. His mind is addled." Well, "addled" means about the same thing as "confused." And I wasn't about to let anyone call me that! I ran right out of the classroom, and didn't stop till I got home.

Mama marched right over to that school and told the Reverend that he must be foolish not to see how smart I was. She decided to teach me herself, since she'd been a teacher before she was married.

I worked extra hard to prove that she had

been right to stand up for me. Every day we sat together and took turns reading aloud from all sorts of books like the Bible and the *History of Rome*. The book I liked best had a long, funny name: *The School Compendium of Experimental and Natural Philosophy*, by Mr. Richard Parker. The *Compendium* was a science textbook. It explained how locomotives and lightning rods and electric batteries worked, and even showed how to build a telegraph machine.

It took me just one day to read *Compendium* from cover to cover. As soon as I finished, I knew I had to put together my own science lab and try out all the experiments that Parker described!

Every week I spent my whole allowance to buy things I needed for my little lab. Pretty soon I had collected over one hundred bottles of chemicals, including ammonia, alcohol, sodium and calcium. I stored them in the cellar.

Mama did her best not to look too worried about all the bottles that I marked POISON! I only used that label so no one would dare to fool around with my experiments. When Papa heard me working in the lab, he'd shake his head and say, "That boy will blow us all up someday!" as if I were another Mad Miller.

Papa decided he had to get me interested in

doing something else. He said he would give me a penny for every good book I read that wasn't about science. That sounded like a terrific idea to me. I'd read everything Papa wanted me to, and spend all those pennies to fix up my lab.

Some of my friends began to look at me a little strangely when they noticed how much time I was spending locked up in a musty basement. But when I let them play with the things I built—magnets, telescopes and magnifying glasses—they saw that science was fun!

Although Papa was a very good carpenter, that wasn't what really interested him. Almost every week he'd come home with the announcement, "Listen everybody! I just had an idea that is going to make us all as wealthy as kings!" Papa's big ideas always sounded wonderful. But as much as he loved to talk about his plans, he never quite got around to trying them out, and the money he dreamed of never came to be. So I went to work just after my twelfth birthday.

I got a job working on the railroad. Six days a week, a shiny, new locomotive chugged all the way from Port Huron to the big city of Detroit and back. I was hired to be that fancy train's newspaper and candy boy. The railroad didn't actually pay me a salary, but I did get to keep a

little money for every newspaper or piece of candy that I sold. "Son," the conductor told me, putting his arm around my shoulders, "your future is up to you. If you're a lazy good-for-nothing, you won't make a plugged nickel on this train. But if you work hard and use your head like the Lord intended, you could make a lot." I decided right then to use my head.

Every day except Sunday, I'd carry my loaded basket through those rolling passenger cars, shouting over the engine's roar, "Peanuts, candy, sandwiches...Get your news, hot off the press!" Either I was a good salesman or a good shouter, because by the end of each trip my basket was empty and my pockets were full of change. My throat was sore, too.

I always had plenty to do. When we stopped over in Detroit, though, I had almost six hours to myself. Luckily, I had thought of a way to pass the time. The baggage car of the train was divided into three sections. I noticed that one of the sections was always empty. That section was too small to hold many suitcases or packages, but it was the perfect size for a lab. I was never one to waste time when I saw an opportunity. I packed up my entire basement lab and moved it into that baggage car.

One day, something terrible happened. I had forgotten to replace the lid on a bottle of phosphorous, a very dangerous chemical. As the train bumped along between stations, some of the liquid phosphorous leaked down from the shelf where I kept it, and burst into flames. I was lucky enough to keep the fire from spreading, but I couldn't do anything about the stink it made. The passengers held their noses and the conductor came running to see if a skunk had climbed aboard. When he saw the mess I'd made, he tossed all of my chemicals off the moving train and gave me the beating of my life!

I was very sorry about that fire, but I was also very stubborn. As soon as I got over crying about my ordeal and the equipment I had lost, I found a way to have fun again in that very same baggage car. It seemed to me that if Port Huron and Detroit had their own newspapers, the Grand Trunk Railway should, too. I bought a tiny old printing press, set it up on the train and made myself the publisher, editor and head writer of the *Grand Trunk Weekly Herald*.

My newspaper was all about the railway and the towns where the train stopped. Whenever the train stopped in a big town, I would jump off with a pile of *Weekly Heralds.* "Read all about the railway, folks," I shouted, "C'mon and get your *Grand Trunk Weekly Herald.*" During one stop, I sold so many papers that I forgot all about the train until it blew its whistle and began to roll down the tracks. I ran after it and grabbed the side of the caboose, but I didn't have the strength to lift myself into the car. I could feel my hands starting to slip. At any moment, I could fall under the train's wheels. I was too scared to even scream.

Suddenly, I felt the trainman's big hands clap against the sides of my head and yank me into the car. I was safe! After a few minutes, though, I noticed something very strange—I couldn't hear a thing! When the trainman had grabbed my head, something inside my ears snapped. When I cried, I couldn't even hear my own sobs.

I'm happy to tell you that it didn't turn out to be quite as bad as all that. My hearing came back little by little over the next few weeks, although it was never quite right again. For the rest of my life I could understand what people were saying if they stood close to me, but the softer sounds, like birds singing and the patter of falling rain, I could no longer hear.

I was definitely not a crybaby, but after my accident, riding the rails didn't seem like such fun anymore. Traveling between Detroit and Port Huron, I felt that I was going back and forth without really getting anywhere. Maybe it was time, I told myself, to find a man's job and a man's trade. Only how could I decide what would be best for me? I was still trying to figure out what job would be right, when suddenly the right job found me!

I was taking a walk one Sunday morning, when I saw the railway telegrapher's little boy, Jimmy MacKenzie, playing on the railroad tracks. He must have been daydreaming because he hadn't noticed that a boxcar had broken loose from the rest of the train and was rolling straight for him! I yelled at him to get out of the way, but he didn't hear me. I took a flying run at the tracks, grabbed Jimmy and rolled out of the way of the oncoming car. We just made it.

When Jimmy's father heard what I had done, he called me a hero and said that I deserved a big reward. "How would you like it," he asked, "if I taught you how to use a telegraph machine? If you turned out to be half as good at that as you are at jumping in front of trains, I could even make you my assistant."

I couldn't wait to begin. Mr. MacKenzie, who insisted I call him Mac, gave me my first lesson the very next Sunday. I suppose I ought to explain that the telegraph at that time was used (and sometimes still is) to send messages from one town to another. This was long before the telephone was invented. Telegraph messages traveled over wires, just like telephone calls do now. But the sounds that went into one end of a telegraph wire and came out the other end weren't voices—they were clicking noises.

A telegraph operator sends and receives messages in something called Morse code. Morse code uses long and short clicks to spell out the letters that form English words. A short click is called a dot, and a long click is called a dash. Take the word "cat." The letter "c" is represented by three short clicks, two clicks one right after the other, then a pause and then the final click, or *dot dot—dot*. The letter "a" is a short click and a long click, *dot dash*. And "t" is just one long click, *dash*. So, putting it all together, "cat" is sent out over the wires like this: *dot dot—dot, dot dash, dash*. It's not all that complicated, but it takes practice.

The telegraph operator would tap out these

18

dots and dashes with a metal key set on a small block of wood. The telegraph turned the dots and dashes into bursts of electricity, and sent them down the wire to a telegraph in another town. When the electric bursts reached the second telegraph, they passed through a device called an electromagnet, which turned them back into long or short sounds. The second telegraph operator would listen to the clicks and convert them into English.

I already knew a little about Morse code from a model telegraph box I'd built in my cellar. Only I couldn't send or receive messages nearly as fast as Mac could. I practiced every Sunday to make myself as fast and accurate as possible. After five months, I became so fast that my tapping sounded as steady as rain hitting a tin roof. "You'd better go tell the railroad to find a new candy boy," Mac said to me one day. "You're coming to work for me!"

The winter of 1864—my first year as a telegrapher—was very cold and windy. During the worst blizzard of the winter, the telegraph cable between Port Huron and Sarnia, Canada snapped. Sarnia was just across Lake Erie from Port Huron, and the two towns did quite a lot of business. When the telegraph broke down, the businessmen couldn't talk to each other to make deals or arrange deliveries of important goods such as oil and coal. They became more and more unhappy.

When I heard about the problem, I went to the railway station manager and told him to bring a locomotive and an engineer to the edge of Lake Erie. As soon as the engineer reached the dock, I climbed aboard. "This is going to be the first train to blow its whistle in Morse code!" I said to the engineer. When the operator in Sarnia heard the long and short blasts from that steam whistle coming across the water, he caught on quickly. After a few minutes, he had another locomotive answering back. We'd started a Morse code conversation between the two engines!

Later on, I received a personal message from the president of the Grand Trunk Railway Company. He'd heard about my quick thinking, and he offered me a job as the night telegrapher in Stratford Junction, Canada. The thought of moving away from my family made me sad, but I knew that they would appreciate the extra money.

Sitting by myself in that station in Stratford wasn't nearly as much fun as working with Mac

had been. In fact, it was boring, since messages hardly ever came in at night. Naturally, I wanted to use the spare time to work on my experiments. But, once an hour, I had to stop what I was doing and tap out the signal for the number "six" (*dot dot dot dot dot dot*) just to let the other operators know that my telegraph was still working.

Being interrupted every hour was ruining my experiments. So I bought a wind-up clock and attached a simple machine to it, which tapped out the signal for six every time the minute hand reached twelve. I was very pleased with myself until my invention got me into terrible trouble. Since I could always count on the "six" machine to make it seem that I was working, I often took naps on the job. One night while I was sleeping, a message came in asking me to stop the 11:15 freight train.

By the time I woke up and heard the message, it was too late. The 11:15 had already passed through the station and was heading straight toward another train! At the last minute, the engineers of the two locomotives caught sight of each other and threw on the brakes. The giant engines stopped just a few feet apart.

The next day I was called to the railway's main office. The general manager stared at me a long time before he suddenly yelled, "Do you realize that people could have been killed because of your laziness? A man could go to prison for less!"

Maybe because I was so embarrassed at what a stupid thing I had done, I didn't quite hear him say that men *could* go to prison—I thought he said that I *would* go to prison! Guilty or not, at fifteen years old, I wasn't ready to be locked up with dangerous murderers and bank robbers.

As soon as I left the manager's office, I ran to my hotel, packed my suitcase and caught the first train back to the United States. I didn't want to go home and explain to my parents what had happened, and lying to them would have been even worse. Instead, I decided I'd take a chance and try something new and really exciting.

The year was 1864, the third year of the Civil War. Most experienced telegraphers had joined the armies of the North or South to help send messages. The telegraphers who were left behind had their pick of jobs. Many of them didn't like to stay in one place for very long. They wandered from town to town and state to state, taking over jobs from the operators who had joined the army. Those fellows were known as "tramp" telegraphers. I decided to join them.

Tramping, as it was called, paid very well. But it also attracted a lot of shifty characters and rough customers. There were retired cowboys, gamblers who had lost their stakes playing cards and even a few people who had fought Indians with the U.S. Cavalry.

The operators I usually traveled with liked to call themselves "lightning slingers," because they said their messages "rode through the lines like thunderbolts." They were a very jolly bunch. Wherever they went, they spent their money as fast as they earned it by staying in fancy hotels and buying fancy clothes or just having fun.

I liked those men, but I didn't want to live as they did. I used all of my extra money to buy special equipment like copper coils and mercury switches, which I needed to teach myself the properties of electricity. So I stayed in the cheapest hotels in every town and wore the same brown suit day after day.

Whenever I tried to think up little inventions

to make the telegraph easier to use, my bosses would say "Do your own job, Edison, and leave the inventing to an inventor!" They were in charge, but I knew that my ideas were good and they couldn't stop me from trying to find them out, especially when no one was watching. I figured they could thank me later, when they saw how much faster I could make their messages fly. Of course, they didn't always thank me. Once, when I tried to build a more powerful telegraph battery, the experiment backfired and I burned a hole through the office floor instead!

When the Civil War ended in 1865, it became more and more difficult for wandering operators to find work. I kept at it for a couple of years more, and then decided that it was time to go home.

It was wonderful to see my family again, but after a few months I couldn't wait to get back to work. Then one day, the boy who was delivering telegrams for old Mac MacKenzie came running to my house with a telegram.

The telegraph message came from a friend of mine named Milt Adams who had been a lightning slinger with me in Cincinnati, Ohio. "I have found a first-class job with Western Union in Boston, Massachusetts," he wrote. "If you can come quickly, I'll have one waiting for you." I took the train to Boston the very next morning.

In those days, Western Union was the world's largest telegraph company, and the operators who worked in their Boston office were considered the best in the business. When those well-dressed city slickers saw my long hair and baggy clothes, they didn't think that I could be much of an operator. They decided to play a trick on me. I was told to sit down and take a message from the New York Western Union office. What I didn't know was that the operator at the other end of the line was the champion telegrapher of the whole company.

Just to catch me off guard, he started out slowly. Then his dots and dashes suddenly speeded up, until he was going so fast that I could hardly keep up! I didn't let the other operators who were grinning behind my back see that, though. I acted as if I thought the New York operator was sending his Morse code very slowly. I even stopped once to sharpen my pencil!

After a long time, the New York operator realized that I had received his whole message correctly and began to slow down. I had won, and I decided it was my turn to have some fun. So I sent him a message saying, "Why don't you send with your other foot now?'' All those slick-ers who had been hoping I'd make a fool of myself roared with laughter. From then on, I was "one of the boys!"

Since Boston hotels were very expensive, Adams and I decided to save money by sharing an apartment. Milt was the only fellow I'd ever known who liked to tinker with electricity as much as I did, so he made a perfect roommate. During the day, we worked side by side at the telegraph office, and every night we squeezed into the little lab in our bathroom and tried out our ideas for improving the telegraph.

The best idea that I ever thought up in that bathroom lab was a special telegraph that could send two separate messages at once. When I perfected my invention, which I called the diplex, it was two weeks before I got up the courage to show it to anyone. Finally, I went to see Charles Williams, a local telegraph maker. My heart was pounding as I demonstrated the diplex to Williams. I knew that it was a useful invention, but I just couldn't help imagining him saying, "This device is worthless," and then sending me on my way. Instead, he didn't say a word. He just walked to his safe and pulled out five crisp one hundred dollar bills and

shoved them into my hand. That was more money than I had ever seen in one place before, and I couldn't have been more excited if it had been a million dollars. Someone had actually paid me to be an inventor!

The next day I sent an announcement to the local paper—"Mr. T.A. Edison has resigned his job at Western Union and will devote all his time to inventing." Now I was off and running! With the money I'd made, I moved into a real laboratory of my own. Over the next few months, I worked on all kinds of interesting inventions. I built an electric fire alarm and an automatic vote-counting machine.

I was expecting to sell the automatic vote-counting machine to the United States Congress. I knew from my telegraph operator days that voting in Congress on a single law sometimes took weeks. With my new machine, it would take only hours. When I brought the vote-counter to Washington to show the senators, I was disappointed to hear that it was, "Just what we do *not* want." As it turned out, the senators wanted the delay in order to get as many congressmen as possible to vote their way.

With no new prospects in Boston, I decided to try my luck elsewhere. I borrowed money and took a boat to New York City. When I arrived, I did not have one cent in my pocket, and the friend I was going to stay with was not at home. So I looked up Franklin Pope. His name was well known at Western Union in Boston. Pope worked for the Gold Indicator Company. He couldn't give me a job, but he let me sleep in the Gold Indicator's battery room and study the indicator, a special telegraph machine called a "gold ticker." It would send subscribers the most current gold prices. The ticker was hooked up to offices all over New York City.

One day, the whole system came to a halt. Subscribers had to send messenger boys to the office to bring back the gold reports that were usually sent over the indicator. Soon, three hundred boys jammed the office. Dr. Laws, the owner of the company, was normally a calm man, but that day he completely lost his head. Even Franklin Pope didn't know what to do. I began looking at the machine and quickly located the problem. Two hours later, the machine was fixed and all the offices were receiving prices again. Dr. Laws offered me a job for three hundred dollars a week!

After a few months of working for Laws, I wanted more freedom. Pope and I formed our own business. We patented a printing tele-graph, as well as other improvements on the telegraph. By now, General Lefferts, the Presi-dent of Western Union, had heard of me. He wanted me to work for Western Union.

General Lefferts had a problem with the machines that printed out stock prices. These machines were similar to the gold tickers and would send the latest stock prices to businesses that wanted them. Once in a while, a machine would run wild and print numbers that were not being sent. It would then have to be shut off and a mechanic had to be sent to repair it. Lefferts wanted me to make the repairs easier. I got to work on the problem. Soon, the central office could fix the machines by sending electrical impulses over the wires, which saved time and money.

General Lefferts and other Western Union officials were very impressed with my idea, so they wanted to keep me happy. Since I had received five hundred dollars for my last inven-tion, I was hoping that this time I might get as much as three thousand. Before I could open my mouth, General Lefferts offered to pay me forty thousand dollars. I nearly fell over when I heard that big number, but I managed to tell him that it would be just fine.

Things cost much less in those days than they do now. A fellow who could put that much money in the bank was rich. It would have been fun to move to a big mansion and eat at fancy restaurants, but the best thing that money could do for me was to help me invent. I used every dollar I'd earned, and even borrowed some, in order to buy a large brick building in Newark, New Jersey, and turn it into my personal invention factory.

Even an inventor needs help sometimes, especially if he wants to get things done more quickly. I hired the best electricians, engineers and carpenters in New York to be my assistants. I have to admit that I wasn't a perfect boss. I made my assistants work awfully long hours. That seemed fair enough to me, since I always worked the longest of all. Some days I didn't even take the time to go home to sleep! Instead, I'd just climb up on a workbench and take a nap.

I would get very frustrated when I had trouble with an invention. When it finally worked, I would be so excited that I would jump up and down and do a little dance.

One day, I was looking out of my office window, and I saw something that nearly made me jump out of my seat! There was a young lady staring right back at me. She was huddled underneath the factory's awning, trying desperately to keep out of the rain. It couldn't have been doing her much good, though, because she was already wet from head to toe. I opened the window and invited her to come in. She came inside then, and thanked me. She said her name was Mary. I thought Mary was the loveliest woman I had ever seen, even soaking wet.

By the time the rain stopped, I knew that I was in love. I was much too shy to ask Mary for a date, so I asked her to come to work for me instead. After Mary had been working for me for a while, I finally got up the courage to ask her out. Well, that worked so well that a few months later I proposed!

Mary and I were married on Christmas Day, 1871, and before five more Christmases had passed, we had two babies. We nicknamed them Dot and Dash. In 1879 we had another son, William.

Meanwhile, I worked two shifts each day at the invention factory, designing things that I hoped would make people's lives a little easier. Some of these inventions were so useful that they are still around today—like wax paper, and the mimeograph machine, which makes copies from one original copy.

After a few years, my assistants and I had filled the factory with so many gadgets that there was nowhere left to work. It was time to build a new lab that would be big enough for all of my new inventions. I knew I couldn't trust just anyone to work on such an important project. It took a person who knew how to dream big to build the great laboratory I had in mind. So I hired my father! At last, my father had a chance to show what he could do. In 1876 he finished my lab in Menlo Park, New Jersey. I thought it was the best in the world.

One of the first inventions I worked on in the new lab was the telephone. A fellow named Alexander Graham Bell had invented the first telephone, but it had some problems. The main trouble with Bell's phone was that the sound it made was not nearly loud enough. Even if a person was calling from only a block away, his voice wouldn't sound any louder than a whisper. That was an especially big problem for a half-deaf fellow like me—I couldn't hear a word!

While I was working on the telephone, I began

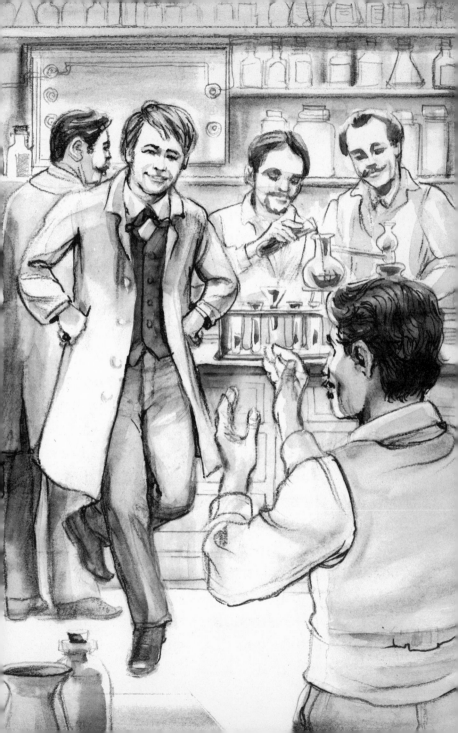

to think that if I could improve a machine that sent voices over a wire, maybe I could also make one that could record voices and play them back later! I put on my thinking cap and made a drawing of a machine that I thought might just do the trick. I gave the drawing to my best mechanic, John Kruesi, and told him to build a model of what I wanted as quickly as he could.

I called the funny contraption I had designed the phonograph. You probably know it better as a record player. That first phonograph wasn't as complicated as the ones you see today, but it could make records, as well as play them. For my first recording on December 6, 1877, I sang "Mary Had A Little Lamb." As I sang, my voice moved the air in front of my mouth, and the air moved a round piece of cardboard called a diaphragm. When the diaphragm moved, it shook a little needle that was attached to it. The point of the needle then cut tiny grooves into a strip of tin foil.

When I had finished singing, there were grooves all over the tin foil that had been made by my voice. I played the record back by running a second needle through the grooves, and the needle shook a second diaphragm. As that diaphragm moved, it shook the air and the moving air made a sound just like my voice.

When John Kreusi heard my phonograph singing "Mary Had A Little Lamb," he looked as if he'd seen a ghost. When the rest of the world found out that I had invented a machine that could record a human voice, folks began to call me the "Wizard of Menlo Park."

I decided I needed a vacation after all the inventing I'd been doing. I joined a group of scientists who were taking a train out west to Wyoming to see a phenomenon called a lunar eclipse. During an eclipse, the moon passes in front of the sun, and it gets dark during the middle of the day. The professors with whom I was traveling were very excited by all that darkness. The eclipse got me thinking instead about how nice it would be if I could make an electric light that would keep things bright all the time.

The idea behind the light bulb was simple, but it was very hard to get one to work just right. When electricity passes through a thin thread of material called a filament, it makes the thread very hot. As the thread gets hotter, it gives off light (just like red-hot coals). The trick is to find a thread that can get very, very hot and give off lots of light, but doesn't burn up or melt.

I tried more than sixteen hundred kinds of filament—everything from spiderwebs to hairs from my assistants' beards—before I found one that burned bright enough and lasted a long time. That day in 1879, I drew a picture of a light bulb in my diary and wrote, "I've won!" in giant letters.

I had a right to be excited, but there was still one little problem. What good was it to have light bulbs that worked by electricity when people didn't have electricity in their houses? Now I had to take care of *that!*

It seemed to me that there was no better place to begin lighting the world than America's busiest city—New York. For almost a year I worked day and night building a huge electric power plant for the city, and laying underground wires to eighty-five of its buildings. On September 4, 1882, when everything was finally in place, I started up the two big steam engines that ran the power plant. The engines rumbled for a few minutes, then suddenly four hundred lamps lit up. I was so excited when I saw all those lights go on that I felt as if the electricity from the plant was running through *me!*

With all my work in New York finished, I finally had time to return to Menlo Park and have some fun with my family. Since I had always loved trains, I built my very own electric railway. The children and I took turns playing engineer as my little train ran in a big circle around the lab. Now, the train was a wonderful toy, but it was also an important invention. The subway trains that run underneath the streets of big cities today all work exactly like my little electric railway.

The year after I returned to Menlo Park, Mary caught a disease called typhoid fever. The doctor told me there was nothing to worry about, and that Mary just needed rest. But every day she rested, my sweet Mary grew weaker. A few weeks later, she died.

My daughter, Dot, who was growing into a beautiful young woman, took care of me. She was very good to me, but I became sadder and sadder. I just moped around the house, and couldn't even bring myself to think of new inventions.

One night an old friend invited me to a party where I met a very pretty young woman named Mina Miller. I couldn't stop thinking about her. I

was falling in love again. A little while after Mina and I met, I taught her Morse code and soon we learned to have private conversations by tapping messages on each other's wrists. One day I tapped, "Will you marry me?" Right away she tapped back, "Yes."

After Mina and I were married, I went to work again. In 1887, I moved my laboratory one last time, to West Orange, New Jersey. The new lab was more than ten times the size of the one in Menlo Park. It was the largest research lab in the world.

In West Orange, I improved the phonograph and invented the first motion picture camera. I also created a machine I called the kinetoscope, which was used to view the finished movies. It was a large wooden box with a peep hole at the top to watch through. I even built a special studio in West Orange to make my movies in. We called it "Black Maria" because it was painted black, inside and out. The roof could be completely opened to let the sun in, or we could use powerful lights. We filmed many different people: dancers, boxers, strong men and even performing bears. What I really wanted was to hook up my movies to the phonograph in order to get pictures with sound. I was very excited when I showed my first talking motion picture.

I also created many other inventions during my forty years in West Orange. There was the wet-cell battery, which helped to run a new machine called the automobile. Then there were the gas masks I made for our soldiers in World War I.

Nobody bothered to tell me that I was getting old. I kept working until I was eighty-four! I'd made a lot of money and could have retired, but I loved inventing and never wanted to stop.

People used to criticize me sometimes. They said I wasn't *really* an inventor because I would never suddenly find a single solution to a problem. Instead, I tried hundreds, even thousands of possible solutions before I found the one that worked. That's why I always said, "Genius is one percent inspiration, and ninety-nine percent perspiration."

When I look back on my life's work, I see that the telephone brought together loved ones who hadn't talked with each other for years. I see that the phonograph put music into people's lives. My fondest memory of all is the electric bulb I created in Menlo Park. With all of my inventions and hard work, I helped to shed some light where before there were only shadows.

The Life and Times of Thomas Edison

1837	Samuel Morse invents the telegraph and the Morse code.
1847	Thomas Alva Edison is born on February 11, in Milan, Ohio.
1854	The Edison family moves to Port Huron, Michigan.
1859	Tom becomes candy and newsboy for the Grand Trunk Railway.
1862	Tom begins the study of telegraphy with J.U. "Mac" MacKenzie.
1864-68	Tom works as a wandering tramp telegrapher, and then becomes a first-class telegraph operator at Western Union's Boston office.
1868	Tom receives his first patent for an electric vote-counting machine, and perfects the gold ticker telegraph. He moves to New York City and improves the printing telegraph for Western Union.
1871	Tom opens his first laboratory in Newark, New Jersey.
1874	Tom invents the mimeograph machine and wax paper.

1876	Tom moves from Newark, and opens a new laboratory in Menlo Park, New Jersey.
1877	Tom improves Bell's telephone with the invention of the carbon button microphone. Tom also begins work on a talking machine, which he calls the phonograph.
1879	Tom perfects the carbon filament for the incandescent light bulb.
1882	Tom brings electric power and light to New York City on September 4.
1887	Tom moves his laboratory to West Orange, New Jersey. Today that laboratory is a museum.
1888	Tom invents the movie camera.
1889	Tom invents the movie viewer, which he calls the kinetoscope.
1901-10	Tom invents the wet-cell storage battery.
1914	World War I begins.
1916-18	Tom invents gas masks, searchlights and smoke screens for the United States Navy.
1931	Thomas Alva Edison dies on October 18.